Grandma Francisca Remembers

Text © 2002 by Ann Morris

Photographs and illustrations © 2002 by Peter Linenthal

Designed by Carolyn Eckert

Other photographs courtesy of © Dave G. Houser/Corbis: p.16;

© Reuters/Daniel Aguilar/Archive Photos: p. 23

Library of Congress Cataloging-in-Publication Data

Morris, Ann, 1930-

Grandma Francisca remembers: a Hispanic-American family story / Ann Morris.

p. cm. – (What was it like, Grandma?)

ISBN 0-7613-2315-5 (lib. bdg.)

1. Hispanic American families—Juvenile literature. 2. Hispanic Americans—

Social life and customs—Juvenile literature. 3. Grandmothers—United States—

Juvenile literature. I. Title.

E184.S75 M68 2002   973'.0468—dc21   2001044086

The Millbrook Press, Inc.

2 Old New Milford Road

Brookfield, Connecticut 06804

www.millbrookpress.com

Printed in Hong Kong

5 4 3 2 1

What Was It Like, Grandma?

Grandma Francisca ❁ Remembers

A Hispanic-American Family Story

Ann Morris
Photographs and illustrations by Peter Linenthal

The Millbrook Press
Brookfield, Connecticut

Angelica with Grandma Francisca

In the middle of San Francisco, California, is a large brick housing project. Angelica, her mother, Anna, and her father, Andres, live in one apartment. Angelica's grandmother, Francisca, lives next door.

Angelica is a happy girl with many friends.

She and her friends often play together in the yard of the housing project. Sometimes they go swimming at the beach.

Angelica also likes reading and going to school. Her school is only a few blocks away. She is becoming an expert on the computer. Someday she would like to work in an office.

Angelica with her best friend, Bianca

Angelica's parents work in a restaurant. Her mother is a waitress, and her father is a cook. Grandma Francisca has many different jobs. She takes care of elderly people, baby-sits, and does housework in people's homes.

Francisca never finished school. Angelica tells her that she should go back to school someday. "It would be fun!" Francisca says.

Angelica enjoys spending time with Grandma Francisca after school and on weekends.

Sometimes they take walks together through the project.
Sometimes they just stay inside.

Francisca's apartment is warm and comfortable.

It is filled with the good smells of Mexican food. Often relatives and friends stop by to visit Francisca and enjoy her good cooking.

Angelica loves talking to Francisca. She also likes it when Francisca fixes her hair.

Angelica and Grandma Francisca enjoy reading together.

Angelica, whose name means "little angel," is learning Spanish at home and at school. Sometimes she practices with Francisca.

Angelica calls Francisca *"mi abuela"* ("my grandmother"). Francisca calls her *"mi fresa"* ("my strawberry") or *"mi sandía"* ("my watermelon").

Francisca says many things to Angelica
in Spanish.

"¿Como te fue en la escuela hoy?"
(How was school today?)
"Te miras muy bonita."
(You look very pretty.)
"Te quiero mucho." (I love you a lot.)
"Feliz Navidad." (Merry Christmas.)
Angelica understands.

Sometimes Grandma Francisca
shows Angelica old family photographs.
She tells her what it was like when
she was little.

Francisca, age three, outside her home
in New Mexico

Grandma Francisca grew up in New Mexico.

She was born in the small city of Chama. Later she and her family moved to Santa Fe and then to Albuquerque. Angelica says, "I'd like to see some of those places where you grew up."

Francisca's father, Frank

Francisca and her mother, Delfina

Francisca has eight brothers and sisters. Her parents were born in the United States, but her grandparents came from Spain.

Her father worked at different chores in people's houses. Francisca tells Angelica that he was called a "yard man." Her mother worked as a cook and cleaning lady for people in the towns where they lived.

There wasn't much money when Francisca was little, but there was a lot of love.

The sisters never called one another by name. Instead, they called one another *"hermana"* ("sister"), which was the custom then. "I love you, sister." "Come here, sister," they would say.

The children called their mother "Mommy" and their father "Papi." All the sisters slept in one room, three in a bed. There was a stove in the bedroom to keep them warm on cold winter nights.

"My parents really understood me," Francisca tells Angelica. "They wanted me to go to school, but they were very poor and always needed money. So I had to work on the nearby farms. Every day I brought a lunch of burritos, coffee, and water to the workers who were digging in the fields. I also helped my mother with the housework."

But, says Francisca, "we had a good life." She and her brother and sisters had a lot of fun playing together and celebrating holidays.

Francisca, age three (second from the right), with two of her sisters and a brother

People dressed for a parade on Three Kings Day

At Christmastime, Grandma Francisca's family celebrated Día de los Reyes (Three Kings Day).

This is a day of gift-giving among many Hispanic people. It honors the three kings of the Bible who traveled to Bethlehem with gifts for the baby Jesus.

Hispanic people often hold parades on Three Kings Day. On this day Francisca's family got together with friends and family and made a delicious meal of fish and *nopales* (cactus plant stems). At night the children put their shoes outside the door. In the morning they found them filled with presents such as hair ribbons, baby dolls, and dried fruit— all wrapped in colorful papers.

Grandma Francisca got married to Grandpa Tony when she was just a young woman.

She soon had one son and two daughters.

When she was twenty-three, a niece who lived in San Francisco told her it was a wonderful place to live. San Francisco sounded so great that Francisca and Tony moved there with their three children.

Francisca as a young woman (right)

with Tony and her mother-in-law

When Grandma Francisca was a little girl, she liked to play
with dolls that she and her mother made together. Now
Francisca shows Angelica how to make the same kind of doll
from a sock and brightly colored buttons.

Angelica loves the doll that Francisca made for her.

Sock Doll

It's easy to make a sock doll.

HERE IS WHAT YOU NEED:

Scissors

Several old socks

Several buttons, in different colors and sizes

Needle and thread

Yarn

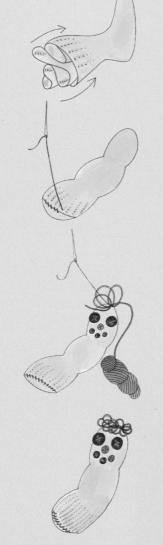

HERE IS WHAT YOU DO:

1. Stuff a sock with several old socks.

2. Sew up the bottom of the outside sock so that the other socks don't come out.

3. Sew on two big buttons for eyes.

4. Sew on a smaller button for the nose.

5. For a mouth, sew a few buttons in a line underneath the nose.

6. For hair, sew several strands of yarn onto the doll's head. The hair can be straight, curly, long, or short.

See how much fun you can have with your sock doll. Make a special blanket for your doll out of a piece of fabric or an old quilt. Give your doll a name— even a birthday! Make different dolls. Make one for a friend.

Good food is something that Angelica's whole family likes.

Sometimes Angelica and Francisca cook stew, tortillas, and other foods together.

Tortillas are a kind of Mexican pancake made from special ground corn mixed with lime. Some people pat tortillas out by hand. Others use a machine.

Making tortillas by hand

Many Hispanic-American people eat tortillas with all kinds of food.

With a little butter they are a delicious snack. They are used to make Mexican-American dishes such as burritos and tacos. Angelica's family often eats tortillas with vegetable stew.

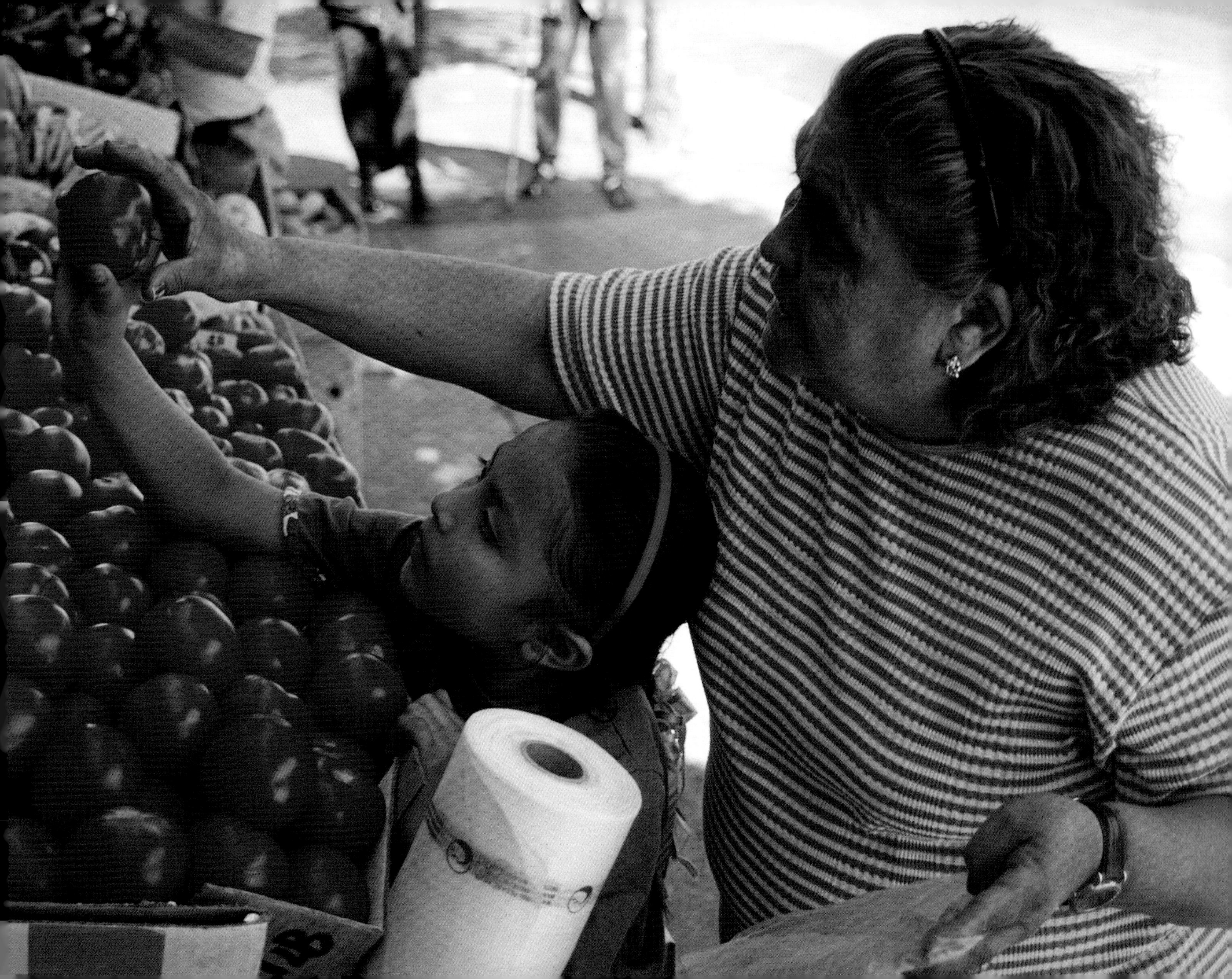

Before they make stew, Francisca and Angelica go to the nearby Hispanic markets to buy what they'll need.

Angelica helps pick out fruits and vegetables.

Angelica is good at cutting up vegetables for Grandma Francisca's delicious vegetable stew.

It is made of tomatoes, zucchini, onion, corn, and garlic.

Calabacitas (Vegetable Stew)

Makes 6 servings

SAFETY TIP:

If you try this recipe, get an adult to help.

HERE IS WHAT YOU NEED:

1 onion, chopped

2 cloves garlic, chopped fine

1 tablespoon cooking oil

2 or 3 zucchini, chopped

2 or 3 ripe tomatoes, chopped

kernels cut from 2 ears corn, or 1 can corn kernels

1 cup chicken stock

HERE IS WHAT YOU DO:

1. Sauté the onion and garlic in oil for 8 minutes.

2. Add the zucchini, tomatoes, corn kernels, and chicken stock.

3. Simmer for 20 minutes.

Enjoy with tortillas or your favorite bread!

Grandma Francisca's family has always been religious.

When the sun goes down, Francisca lights up a shrine in the hallway. She explains that her altar is like the one her mother had. In the center is a statue of the Virgin Mary. Around the statue Francisca has placed family photographs, candles, and flowers.

The Virgin Mary, the mother of Jesus, is very important to Hispanic people. They pray to her for many things. Grandma Francisca and her mother used to pray to the Virgin Mary and the Father every day. They asked them to help the sick and lonely people they knew.

Now Francisca and Angelica do the same thing. As the lights of the shrine glow softly, they pray together in Spanish. "Santa Maria y Padre Nuestro. . . ."

Angelica with her Grandma Francisca and her mother, Anna

All About My Family

Would you like to know about your family? Here are some things you can do.

INTERVIEWS

You will find out many interesting things about your relatives by interviewing them. Ask them questions about their childhood—where they lived, what they liked best to do and to eat, what they read and studied in school. Find out, too, how things are different today from when they were young. Use a tape recorder to record your questions and their answers.

FAMILY ALBUM

Ask your relatives for pictures of themselves. Put all the pictures in an album. Write something you have learned about each person under his or her picture.

FAMILY TREE

All of us have many relatives. Some of us are born into the family. Others are related by marriage or have been adopted. You can make a family tree that looks like the one on the next page to show who belongs to your family.

Morales Family Tree

Francisca

Tony

Anna

Angelica

Andres